when Supernova dies

elena lycette

© Copyright, when Supernova dies, 2021 elena lycette

All rights reserved. No part of this publication may be reproduced, stored in or introduced into a retrieval system, or transmitted, in any form, or by any means (electrical, mechanical, photocopying, recording or otherwise) without the prior written permission of the publisher. Any person who does any unauthorized act in relation to this publication may be liable to criminal prosecution and civil claims for damages

Lycette, Elena
    when Supernova dies / by Elena Lycette.
Sacramento : I Street Press, 2021

   ISBN: 978-1-952337-48-2

   Library of Congress Control Number: 2021920636

   Copyright registration number: TXu002242963

Cover Design by Julia DeNecochea

Printed in the United States of America

I Street Press
828 I Street
Sacramento, CA 95814

dedicated to TBJ
december 16, 1993 - november 7, 2018

for the reader

it was the end of summer 2017, i was nineteen years old attending my second year at american river college. i met him in front of the brick wall of our english writing class. we sat right next to each other; our eyes knew each other and i listened for his name every single day. time didn't exist here. it wasn't long before we were engaged. while he taught me life, i experienced what it meant to be alive. our adventures were between the ocean of the bay and the lake of the mountains, between suburban homes and city buildings, between our bed and the hospital beds, between our grocery store and the pharmacy, between the freeway and the cemetery, between life and death. TBJ had sickle cell anemia and he never shared his illness with anybody. he was an intellectual, a writer, an athlete, a dear friend, a family man, a man of faith, a lover, and a thoughtful person. he died on a wednesday morning during the fall of 2018, the day before the california wildfires raged. TBJ had three open caskets and was buried in the afternoon of winter, exactly one month from the day he died, before his twenty-fifth birthday. the coroner report arrived in the spring of 2019. i attended a bereavement group, therapy and counseling. i was diagnosed with ptsd during the summer of 2019. my college experience was altered and my life transformed. i became a different person when he died and i lived, and i want you to live. if these words help you to heal then my words and painful experiences will carry a meaning beyond myself. i put my pain into poetry and i did not hide myself in the art. i hope you allow yourself to feel the emotions that may arise throughout this book. i hope my path is the hand of a teacher. i challenge you to face the fear of your own mortality and create grace in the unpredictable reality of life. i am writing this now, two years later in the winter of 2020, and i promise you that there is more life to experience since he died. Supernova is a star that can take billions of years to die, its explosive light can be witnessed after its death. this is a collective of poems from the first year of losing TBJ. this is what happens when Supernova dies.

timeless

you're always worried
we are running out of time
if we could break the
numbers into colors
we would find that
time is blossoming around us
and the only thing left
of time
turned into art
and music

chapters

welcome 1

november 2018 3

december 2018 17

january 2019 35

february 2019 49

march 2019 69

april 2019 77

may 2019 89

june 2019 101

july 2019 115

august 2019 129

september 2019 145

october 2019 153

november 2019 167

TBJ 2017 - 2018 183

acknowledgements 195

welcome

it's going to get morbid
it's going to get sexual
it's going to get painful
welcome to the darkness of my mind
you've been cordially invited
to witness my broken
beautiful reality
in this dimension called life

november 2018

WEDDING BAND

i do

we spent our nights holding hands
next to the ocean waves
watching the stars and the moon
i was always afraid of the ocean
but there was you
you made my fears fade
and i threw myself into you
i lived for you
and i still do

twin bed

my skin is hard like cracked desert
these tears dried like glue
from the loss of you
i hate living
would you share your bed with me
to rest indefinitely?
'til death we part
'til afterlife we?

melted glaciers

the truth is
we thought we were invincible
death happened to people around us
but it would never happen to us
we could love the illness out of each other
until it crushed under the weight of our bodies
as we made love into the night
until the cold weaved its way into your covers
and pain made its last debut
i thought you would never die
i thought you were more alive
when you died
i stopped dreaming about tomorrow
nothing was real to me
life went on without you
and i felt the pull from your soul in limbo
beckoning me to take your hand
for so long i loved death
i didn't appreciate life
i loved you like the waves love the moon
you pulled me into you
and made my glaciers melt
i didn't care if the world drowned
i just wanted to flood until you could see me
i feel like distance is death
i feel like promises are lies
and love is the only reason why
we choose life every time
i choose you
even if it kills me

something you once told me

"we're not special
everyone dies"

california wildfires

the day after you died there was fire
we were enveloped in smoke
it burned our lungs and our eyes
but i couldn't tell the difference
from the salt dripping from my eyes
all that was left of us was smoke
i could feel mother earth burning
she was a fire that wouldn't die

casanova

we would drive through hills and mountains
through bridges and oceans
i'd watch the city lights
thinking of the man you were before i knew you
wishing i knew you then
so i could have loved you longer

a place called heaven

he took me to this place called heaven
it's on top of a hill
it overlooks the homes where we had plans
plans to spend our lives together
it's called heaven here because you can see the stars
i'm still convinced he brings down the moon for me
he was a private man
but he shared the world with me

cliffhouse beach

we saw the ocean at night
picking up seashells and talking about beauty
and where it resides
was it the way the moon pulled the waves
or was it the way the wind pulled us closer together?
i'm still listening for your voice

painful healer

you made me realize
that pain is necessary in life
it makes us humble
it makes us humxn
it made you alive in every way

healthcare should be free

i remember many nights we spent at the hospital
but i wasn't afraid of you
your illness did not define you
because you were so much more

i'm honored to be your last love

you gave me a love that cannot be confined
to the limitations of time

eulogy pieces

he had dreams
his dreams are still alive
he built a home in us wherever he went
he is not in pain anymore
his dreams never died

december 2018

MORNING CALM

three open caskets

love is an ocean
reality ripped me out of the sheets
the sheets they used to cover your body
the covers we used to make love in
the covers that float over me in my dreams
i'm pretty fucked up since you died
my mind is a dark and twisted mess
like a rose wrapped in thorns
sometimes i'm afraid that there's something wrong
with me
i feel like everything i touch dies
like everything i love is going into oblivion
i'm so empty i read to fill the space
hoping these words will lead me to you
to me
to a love that doesn't die
ever since you died i have chosen to live
even when i am tempted to end the pain
i choose to embrace it
to feel it deeply
and to love me
to love life
despite its darkness
i will live for the both of us

six feet under

in my dreams since you died
your casket is filling with water
and nothing i do can stop you from decaying
and nothing i do can stop our poems from washing
away
our art disintegrated
your body floated
you're so beautiful to me
i can't believe you're decomposing beneath me
before you died i'd dream of the ocean
i'd dream of the flood
of the tsunami
nothing i did could stop it
i was trapped behind glass walls
watching the waves rise six feet higher
i wish you still lived here with me
laying on the sand
making love next to the crashing waves
telling me that my nightmares were only dreams
wake me up babe
i think something bad is going to happen

the womxn you loved has died

i can't believe reality
it has poisoned my heart
made me dark inside
i prefer to live in your dimension
bury me alive
and pour the earth in my body
for the womxn you loved has died
she rests within a dimension
written in past times
she lives in your arms
everyday eats at my core and haunts my mind
i wish that life could have been simple
no hospital beds or pain
i wish that our love never dies

burial grounds

**i hope that your spirit doesn't feel confined to this space
you are free my love and you are loved**

portals of my mind

how can it be?
that when your pain ended
mine began

heaven is an idea

everybody is waiting for heaven
but what if there is no heaven?

past lives

**i wish that i had a lifetime with you
but even that wouldn't have been enough for us**

3:33pm december 7th

**we knew the reality of your illness
but still you died**

hope is a rope

we talked about death almost every other day
i feared it while you faced it
the reality was clear
yet we held onto love dearly
we chose each other
who am i without you?

suppression

i wanted to knock over the flowers
shake your casket
and scream into your cavities
why won't you wake up?
this nightmare isn't ending
i wanted to climb into your tomb
please let me be buried right next to you
let me lie here with you
i don't care if your body is cold
i don't care if you smell like poison
you are my lover
and i wish it had been my time to go
so i could have spent my whole life with you

death is selfish

**and when we are gone
we leave pain all around us**

traumatic cycle

while everyone is moving forward
i still live in yesterday
i relive the day you died
over and over again
i remember my steps
i remember the clocks
i remember my hands shaking
the paths i took
i remember the stairs
i remember seeing your socks first
our blankets over your body
your face
and the teardrops
the color of your eyes
your beautiful body

shameful healing

all i feel is pain
anything that isn't will feel like
shame

pulling out the weeds

let me tell you what it's like
to love a man who is dead
for sex to constantly intoxicate your mind
and his body is a poison i can't live without
i want to drink him until i no longer feel empty inside
but his body is sealed shut
and he isn't hard because he wants me
he is frozen in time
decomposing under the earth
with pieces i left in his tomb
if he could see this he would know he owns me
for i feel shame at the thought of anyone else
i wish he could drink my milk and fertilize my garden
i was always the delicate flower
wet petals and delicious pollen
he stung me like a bee
and he took everything beautiful about me
i grew thorns to save me
i'm not ready for spring to come
wet petals for me to bathe in
delicious pollen to embrace
milk flows endlessly
my garden is growing more flowers
and i'm pulling out the weeds
the warning of the seeds
do not let the dead overstay their welcome
or weeds and sharp thorns will gather
and tempt you to touch them
while bees collect pollen and nectar
the dead spills blood and drains you empty
until you're nothing
but a body in a bag

remember

sex turned into violence
blood dripping on your leather seats
love turned toxic
i drank your elixir
eternal lovers
our lungs were fire that starry night
your eyes were both the angel and the devil

the haircut

the new me cut her hair
and wore black
she doesn't want to look back

january 2019

of triumph hopefully i can change the world as i change myself i love a woman who is incredibly painful but it only breaks you down until you are both strong and broken mind as a girl living a happy and ordinary life only gave me purpose it gave me bruises that somehow i know that even when i am a caterpillar but somehow a butterfly art and it gave me my life as an ordinary-be healed woman through time my music my relationships were beautiful but it was no longer ordinary and at times it was and with change there is adversity bruises and thorns crawl up and down i dream of change i am alone i am capable of love and capable

Elena Lynette DelaRochea ♡

be proud of your life

people will walk in and out of your atmosphere
made not to heal you
but to teach you

he isn't coming home to me

i find myself feeling free
when i forget what i have lost
when i close the doors
and let go of what was never mine

i forgot you died

**i still wake up confused
maybe one day i will wake up next to you
surprised you are alive**

shell of a man

this world is material
you were personal to me
then you left the doors and the windows open
the keys became useless
you weren't coming home
i'm left with your belongings
they smell of you
but they aren't you
i curl up to shells of you
and whatever is left of you
there is no meaning anymore

the void in me

the view doesn't lift me
the music doesn't comfort me
the art doesn't connect me
the space doesn't give room
the people don't fill the space
whatever darkness lives in me
has taken all that is beautiful
and left me feeling like an empty shell

split thoughts

i pray for infection
i pray for disease
i pray for an accident
to split my thoughts into ease
your death has the power to dismantle me

blood at the seams

i cut myself
to see if i could still feel anything
you're dead and maybe so am i
am i worthy of death?

reasons i hate jesus

your casket was your favorite color
dark blue
the words beloved son on each corner
i still have the plaque from your casket
i owe it to your father's kindness
the flowers were white roses
the last roses you ever gave me
they put jesus with you twice
one wrapped around your hand
the other on your chest
you always loved jesus
we argued about him all the time
while you gave jesus your pain
i gave him my anger
it's easier to take it out on the dead

the viewing

i remember feeling ill
driving to your viewing at the cemetery
i hadn't seen you in weeks
not even in my dreams
then i felt faint walking up those steps
the urge to scream through the silence
to ditch my heels and run through moving traffic
world hear my rage
the man i love has died
i wanted to break down the doors and run to you
i was scared of you
your parents went first
that was hard to accept
i felt like you were mine
but you were only mine for a short time
you were their baby for an entire lifetime
i waited and time passed instantaneously
i began to walk towards you
i imagined a hallway first
there wasn't
there was you on display for the world to see
i don't remember who opened the doors
i don't remember who ushered me to go inside
i remember your face and your hands
you looked so different to me
i almost didn't recognize you anymore
i fell to my knees shaking
i dropped the box
the gifts i would share with you forever
worried you might forget about me
worried you might need pieces of me
to help you sleep alone for an eternity
i was crying
and my tears kept landing on your beautiful suit
your father's clothes

your mother sat next to me
and we held each other crying into you
your father stood and held onto your mother
looking at you
his son
i felt the poison in you
the formaldehyde used to preserve you
how strange that where blood pumped in your veins
now lived a poison sicker than your illness
this smell lived in my chapstick
my tights
your makeup left stains on my lips and my fingertips
i rejected everything i saw
the only part of you i accepted as real
we once planned
that my cremated remains would be buried with you
but you died when i was only twenty-years old
i had no ashes to give to you
and the ring was your size
i thought there would be music or wedding bells
there was silence and overwhelming sadness
it still lives in me

gutted

i'll spend my whole life searching for you
never finding you in other people

february 2019

IN BLOOM

milk into tea

in your loss i found me
no husband or maternal journey
i made a womb out of my dreams
and i made my milk into tea
my tears into sacred baths
thank you for loving me
your death set me free

"write about us"

a tree's roots buried underneath the earth
to break that life line
that love transcending earth and time
romeo and juliet would leave us both dead
who would live to tell our story?

sharing grief

life is a seed that grows
a flower that wilts
dead roses
wet petals
a path without direction
a year without summer
a series of betrayals
a transformation from within
a child you learn to forgive
a mothering of self
a reflection of bruises
a life is personal
and i chose to share it with you

group therapy

i would like to imagine that you're proud of me
that you like the womxn i am becoming
i would like to imagine you never died
i would give up half my life to split with you
here on earth
where your beautiful mind undressed me
your laughter flooded my atmosphere
your touch
there are no words to describe
i find group therapy helps
if it weren't for people like us
who spoke the language of loss

he would die before me

we cried together
wiping tears off of each other
and holding life so close
he looked in my eyes so deep
"all i ask of you
is that you publish my book when i die"
i promised him
and the promise is the only thing
that hasn't died

yesterday my tears watered your flowers

i have to release
or i will end up being
the ashes in your soil
and the flowers will curl up and die
i cut my hair
i changed my clothes
i left this place
and it wasn't because i didn't love you
it's because i love you
that it destroys me so deep
the only way out is to live
and to transform the outside in
until the clocks break babe
i will never love again

blank canvas

**it's amazing to me
how colorless my world has become**

permanent relocation

he packed the suitcase of meaning
vacated the body i curled into

loss is surreal

the house plans i drew live in a box
you divided us
you never knew my dreams
marriage was never meant for us

blued

today i'm not here
i'm not real
i exist between walls closing in on me
why am i trying to find myself again?
lost within a path that always veers
trees that i planted
flowers that i bloomed
rivers that i cried
skies that i blued
i went pink in my hues
under the grace of you
i am grey within the limbo
pull me closer
and i'll destroy my dreams for you
i'd give up changing the world for you
no use in stitching my cuts together
when i'm the one using the blade
you can't help me babe
watch my dreams catch fire
my life is a hell that you can't water

oblivion

smoke my lungs
drink my liver
water my veins
crush my flowers
burn my tongue
steal my air
cut my hair
paint my face
shave my legs
rip my clothes
cry my river
scream my throat
light my moon
dark my sun
empty my space
circle my nipples
cut my wrists
sell my body
steal my dreams
bury my lover

no appetite

**i want to starve myself
until the hole in my chest
matches the empty of my belly**

it was god's plan

god didn't like me
and i didnt like him

i hate people

**i'm not happy with the living
they don't live for me**

mind poison

how you destroy me without words
without touch
i throw stones and rip sheets and break glass
the lust to be taken by your gaze
i can't fill the void
it's turned into cancer
flowers wilting
petals dropping
tears become rivers here

muddy heels

can you see my face?
the lines of distress held up with grace
his body beneath my legs
my heels sink into him
the gravity here is deep

i am your lover

i traveled to the deepest parts of your grave
i went deep into the hole where your body lay
i went into your closet
inhaled your body on the clothes
i went into the darkest places of your phone
uncovering secrets never told
arguments between myself and the ghost of you
i went into the deepest parts of my mind
so alive it felt like illness
i danced with your spirit
and made love with you in my dreams
i drove to the ocean and the tallest peak
went to the earth without time to reflect
i bathed in your loss
and it stuck to my skin like thick nectar
everybody wanted a taste
but i closed every window
and locked every door
i put the key in your pocket
and whispered the answer in your ears
i am your lover
always near
while everyone moves on
i am still here
how is love like this fair?

march 2019

IT IS WELL

cut flowers

i filled myself with you
i made my dreams from your seed
only to be cut and displayed
in a vase filled with poison water

barber

he would cut his hair over the sink
his lines were perfect
he never took me with him to the barber
he didn't like other men looking at me

the coroner called

i am so fucking overwhelmed
how can i blame you
for the things you can't explain?

tights in trash bins

i remember i couldn't be alone
for more than five minutes
i'd start screaming and throwing things
in your parents i could hear you sometimes
i'd hold onto your bed and fall asleep
cry on your sheets
smell your clothes and fold them
body on hangers
we chose clothes to bury you in
i cleaned your room
set up your awards and accomplishments
spoke to people i never knew
went to two different types of therapy
called the hotline so many times
i lost count
struggled to run
ten pounds emptier
i never left your side
and so i smelled like death through my tights
it never washes out

god is dead

nope
i'm sorry
but god is not listening
you don't think i tried banging on his door?
screaming into his air
filling his ears with my anger and fear
you don't think i tried praying on my knees?
while my lover lay next to me
breathing eyes closed
lashes fluttering
chest rising
you don't know what it's like
to spend a whole year of your life
between hospitals beds and mountains
between iv drips and oceans
between pills and bridges
between illness and love
it took up so much space
the stars made room
the planets were silent
and then you died
i cried while you slept
with flowers hanging from your veins
we never talked about your illness
to the world around us
but between us it always tried
to divide us
we knew that everything could crumble in an instant
we knew that our love was not enough
to stop the flood from drowning us
i would have given anything to keep you alive
god doesn't answer me
you made promises
so did i
god is dead to me too sometimes

so please stop telling me to pray and to have faith
the universe gave up on us
my only dream is my lover and i
making up for lost time

april 2019

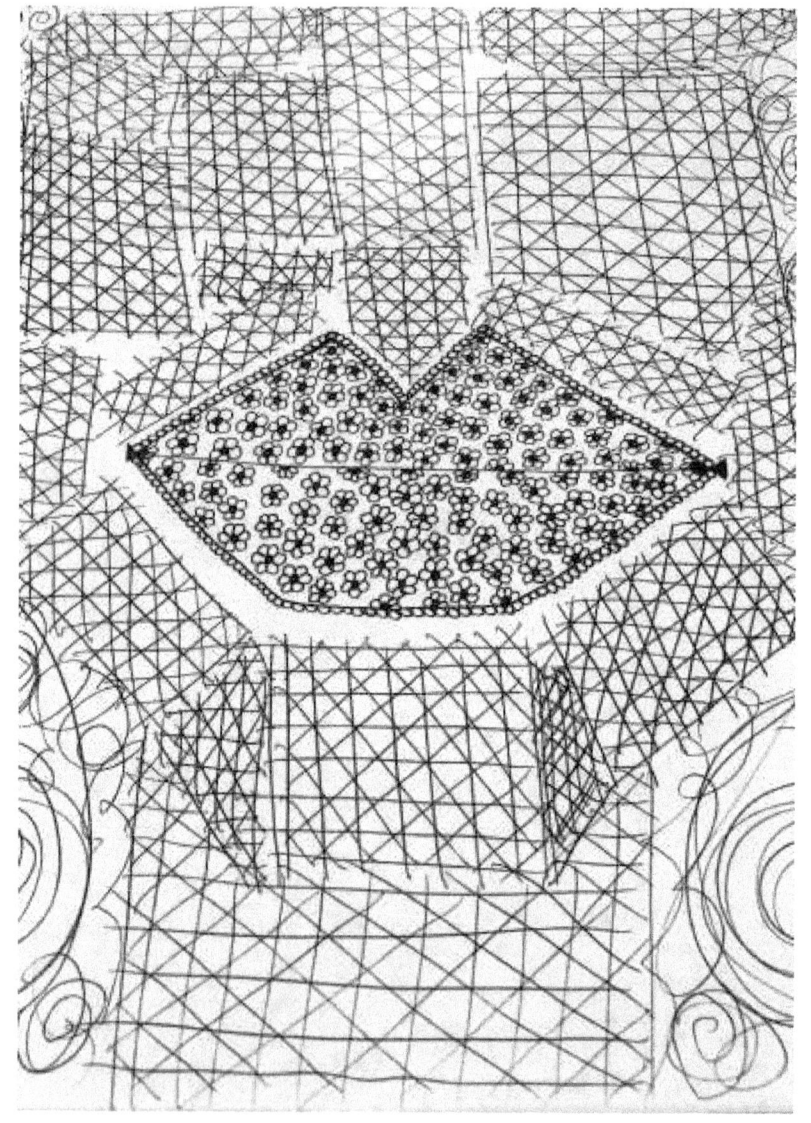

cleaning your room

there are pieces of my memory
that i boxed away
i protected myself
from a pain that was flooding me
i remember pieces
and i remember how still the air felt
it lacked your presence
it carried my fear
it reflected my pain
when you died
i cleaned your room and i folded your clothes
i smelled your scent in the sheets
and i held back every tear
it was all a dream and i could now disappear
i organized your books and your papers
i pulled your trophies onto shelves
and dusted away the past
disinfected the illness
and felt the anger ripping inside of me
i wanted to break your things
and scream into the stillness
your absence was so cold
i wanted to know love was still real
i put your life into drawers
and onto plastic hangers
i felt the past beckoning me
i felt the waves pulling me under
i loved you and i still do
what happened to those dreams?
those plans on paper
i am haunted by your loss
i still visit you
never ask why

cemetery chimes

every month i bring you flowers
i go alone to hear my thoughts
be in tune with my emotions
i am not alone when i am near you
the only sound comes from the wind
it breaks me to come here
i will never let your peace be disturbed
or your memory forgotten
flowers are the only gifts i can bring
you can't know the timeline
you'll never know when the world unfolds
but you can trust in this moment

dying young

you decompose as i grow older
your dreams unfinished
mine just beginning
nothing is fair
between the dead and the living

the burial

flooded mind
i'm crying into my mother's arms
at your cemetery
i feel my heels sink
i weep your loss so deep
i am more numb than empty
i am not ready to bury you

awaken self

everything was so traumatic and painful
an emotional wavelength
a dark hole i was being pulled into
i can't remember most of it
my mind protected me
and buried everything deep within me
there's pieces of the trauma that come back to me
they feel distant
i almost want to hold myself
tell her that with pain there is a joy that follows
eventually you start living again
you wake up to yourself and feel whole again
i allow myself to feel worthy of this life
of this love you and i created
nothing replaces you
will you be a stranger to me when we meet again?
nothing changes who you are to me

alive

i'd love you again
knowing it would destroy parts of me
i will feel my pain and not try to medicate it
or cut it out of me
or sink it so deep i end up burying me
no i will not feel nothing
i am not dead
i am alive and so i shall feel everything
even when the pain is deep
i am grateful to feel anything
to feel is to be alive

sincere

your love was not meant to drown me
and it wasn't meant to destroy my life
your love was so sincere
it gave me open doors

beyond gravity

i drive through scenes of our life
moments shared
even in the present moment
the past is fluid
it beckons me to feel you close
i can feel your touch
my memory is not failing me
we are made to experience
something that is beyond gravity
and when i think of your kiss
i get lost in my dreams
i cannot continue
to sink deeper into the dirt
i am not dead
i die more everyday
after breathing i will know
a different dimension
where answers are not important anymore

healing hands

therapy saved my life
and i am finally in a space
where my thoughts can speak
my hands can heal
my tears can dry
i allow myself to feel again
everything is better than nothing
i am not going to fight myself anymore
there is no home within the war
i had no choice but to keep living
i am so in love with myself
i have the power to heal
never thought i'd find myself again
but she's always been here
i continue to look inward
and care for the child in me
let go of taming the wild within me
i love the womxn i am becoming

may 2019

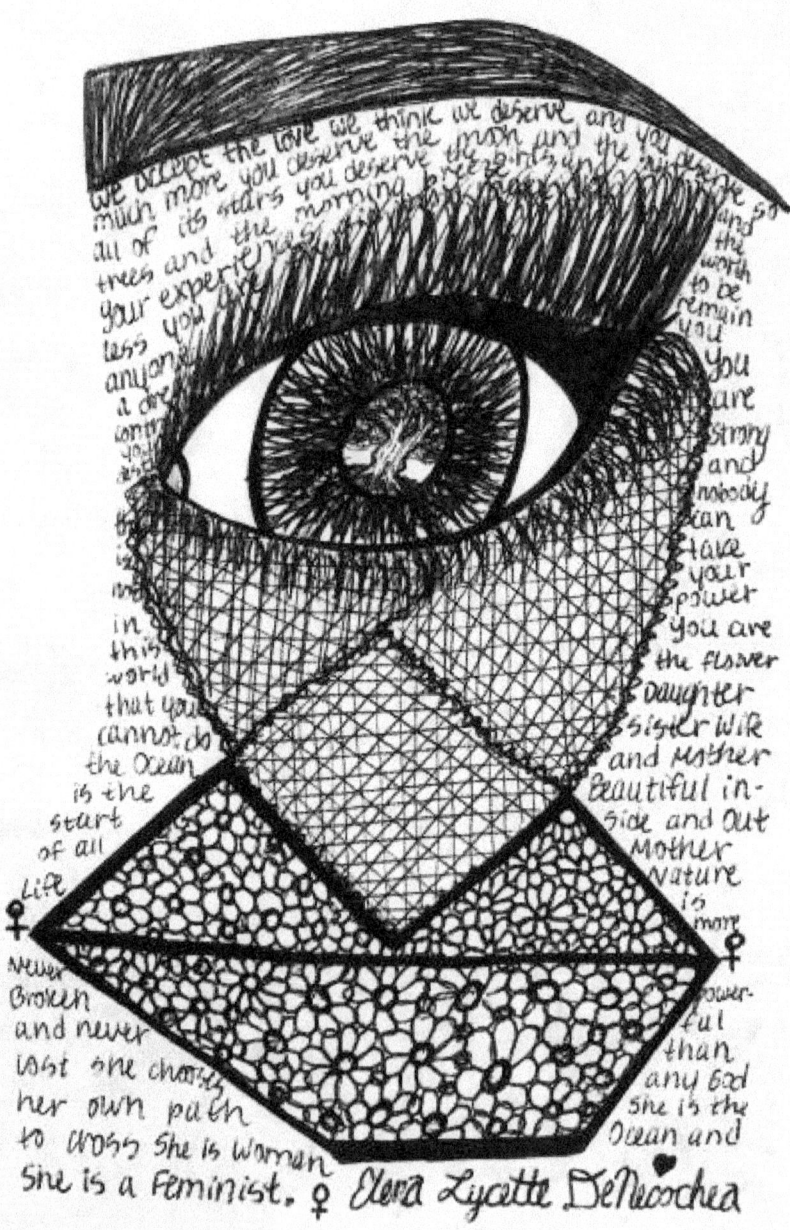

generational secrets

we look at our past selves with distance
the child weeps but we don't come near
it's almost like we worked so hard
to get to this place where peace reigns
we forget the world is suffering
that we were once alone too
you hold the secrets to generations of pain
share these secrets

the weight of living

you left laundry in the basket
the beamer collected dust
the book sat on the shelf
my birthday candles were dim
your mother needed flowers
you're not here anymore
i am cleaning your room
folding your clothes
the beamer needs a wash
the book isn't published
i cried on my birthday
i bring your mother flowers
i wish you were still here
it's not my responsibility
to live your life for you
but live for you i do
there is work to be done
i won't die
please come back to me

bilingual

**language became a barrier
twisted tongues**

more horror

i sleep so often
to fill the silence in the room
i can hear the fan move
but i can't silence my thoughts
distant dark nights
where the wind crawled up my spine
the cold lived in my neck
i didn't have the words to explain
didn't have the legs to run away
you showed me something
that was more horror than violence
i tried to cut it out of me
you buried me too and i still loved you
something beautiful
is something wrong?

the staircase

i walked through the void
ran up the stairs
saw your body on the floor
blanket covering your face
on my knees
pupils burst
teardrops dispersed
i was afraid of you
i wasn't ready
i'm still not ready
someone end me
before my mind destroys me

suicide hotline

between you and i
i don't want to be here anymore
oh how good it feels to say that
to feel my words
please
release what's cultivating deep within me
i fooled you all
into believing i was getting better
you wonder why i don't leave my bed
everyday i am diseased
i am someone else
it's scary to me
i'm traumatized
poisonous thoughts
where i drift between what will become of me
and what i can do to end me
i am not really me anymore

everything hurts

i thought death split us
it was you

withdrawals

you were sick
and i didn't know the sickness in your head
only the one we shared in your bed
i'm sorry if i let you down
i'm sorry you had to hide this
you were more than your illness
i love all your good
i love all your bad
and i forgive you everyday

hotel rooms

maybe i'm what's keeping you here
maybe you can't leave when you see me
all made up taking my heels off
sliding into a hotel bed
feeling empty inside
drinking rose colored bottles
using tv sound to fill space

june 2019

Crying because... Blunt on Fire

she

she's the paint across the sky
the riptide across the sea
the wind outside the car window
the stars painting the empty
the liquor spinning in your cup
the smoke between your lips
the blood in your teeth
the purple in your bruises
the sex in your bed sheets
the bubbles in your bathtub
she's the love of your life

single

**i won't feel guilty
i am free to feel pleasure instead of pain**

baptism

i might say something
that alters your dimension
breaking the hands of time
i could let silence fill the space
create the reality i seek
painting lavender skies around me
feeling naked
under the weight of the night around me
i run from feeling
painting blue blood onto these wrists
drinking the empty that fills me
smoking the rage inside of me
until the clouds make it harder
for you to see me
i'm afraid of being naked around you
wishing you could know how dark my world was
i scream until i cried
breaking glass to feel anything at all
i am worthy
world you don't own me
fuck your holy words
and your sinner mind
i bathed in the water
i let the fire come inside
and i will live before i die
the only thoughts i have
are words i wrote on paper
tattoos that wrap around my art
called body
your love never defined me

i do not need you

i don't exist to fill space
or make you feel needed
i am forgiving who i was before
and still loving her the same

love is worthy of us

feelings of inadequacy
poisoned the relationship
i wish i was the addiction of the addict
i am positive
that love alone does not fill cracks
all are worthy of love
love is worthy of us

success is lonely

my success is not dependent on others
i feel joy and i bathe in it

(p)eople (t)hat (s)ee (d)eath

choose your reality lovely
slip into the silence of your mind
quiet your darkest visions
make space for new beginnings
plant flowers in the dead
make love in your bed
whisper words unsaid
if people could see the things you've seen
they would never be the same
call it ptsd
people that see death
a trauma that keeps your mind from resting
you can't sleep so you drive all night
you cry and fantasize
about crashing into the divide
you see reality for what it is
put your feelings in a box
let the pain subside
i can't make the fear take a backseat
it lives in my body
so i don't care about what the world thinks
if i need a smoke i'll drag it deep
if i need to drive
i'll go until the sun arrives

am i dead too?

you're just gone
you're a deep darkness
a wound that doesn't heal
i'm afraid of you sometimes
when i dream of you i know you died
i think maybe i'm dead too

celebrate life

it's not my time to go
i have so much life inside of me
flowers blossoming
petals around me
maybe we are celebrating
so bring the stars and the moon
it's time to dance
unveil the unknown
break the hands of time
give me more
i'm not done here
i want more life
more love
don't deprive me
i choose to be something great

goddess

i bathe under the sun
throwing my legs into the light
lifting my back off the earth
bending against gravity
giving myself to the stars
i feel a breeze folding my hands into peace
i'm dancing and there's no music
making art without colors
i've learned to awake the night
my voice gets louder every time

puzzle pieces

like a puzzle
the pieces are starting to fit again
many mistakes were made
and i tried to make art
even when it wasn't meant to be
i tried to force pieces
that folded under the pressure of my mind
i watched the story that would become of me
and i finally could make sense
of the art i was creating
it took time
all masterpieces do
my mind grew
and finally
my hands can create again

july 2019

love needs space

maybe i can experience
a love that gives me space

ballerina

i hope it brings you peace
seeing me dance again

reincarnate him

**i hope you're born again
i hope the dead will live again**

broken wider

pain you are not useless
you have been a teacher
you broke my heart
split it wider
now i have more to give

making love with shadows

my past cannot be used as a tool
to hurt me
to redefine me
to destroy me
my past no longer exists here
it's behind me
it has led me here
and it is respected

abortion

sometimes i feel like
men love the idea of me
the idea of a wife and a baby
i alone am not the love they seek

wasted womxn

naked under my satin slip
i'm smoking to die sooner
i've cut my skin into scars
no one could love the broken in me
not even me
you feel empty so you drink me
your drunk and then you don't want me
i'm a bottle you shattered
against the wall
for a world that doesn't want me
i wish death would choose me

cracked

spirit says here are the cracks
fill them
i am humxn
i did what i had to do to survive
i wore a mask and played a role
knowing that i made it here

a poet with no name

what if i was brave enough to be happy?
to smoke without shame
smear lipstick into mascara
dance into who i have always wanted to be
could i be okay with the outcome of my life?
i always wanted to be remembered
i am no one special
just another life well lived

mother moon

i'm ripping up the sky
blue tears lavender
pink evades the atmosphere
exposes the stars
planets spin alive
i'm driving through these empty roads
we have so much in common
we fill the darkness with music
the stars whisper truths
splitting the future from the past
the moon follows us
the mother of our emotions
she drains the sea when she is empty
fill the empty i scream
blood in my veins
i cut open the truth
the scar is the sacrifice
i run until my lungs rip inside
i hold the weight of my dark mind
and i make love with flowers that grow
until the seed plants inside
life goes on
let the pain break you
so you may seek higher truths
reflections alter
mind bends to the waves of ocean water
rolling emotions onto shore
even in another lifetime
i couldn't have known everything
the cycle repeats
we must learn
and you couldn't prepare for this
darkness will smoke you into ash
you are not empty
you are alive

bend into prayer
bathe your spirit
combat the darkness

ex-boyfriend

i love you but you empty me
you gave darkness a home
it made me numb
please cut it out of me

august 2019

ELLA ROSE

eve

**self love is a garden
you must water**

salt water

never abandon self
healing is an ocean
salt in the wound

choose yourself

arguments are not normal
leave as soon as you want to

room in pieces

what peace did you gain
at the loss of me?

no violence

people leave
and they don't come back
it's okay
let them leave

open wounds

right now she's telling me to cut deeper
i'm afraid if i do i'll never stop
because opening wounds
is like opening doors to the past
allowing that pain to own you
dismantle you
my home
my progress
i won't let you
touch me like that anymore
your violence is not love

ivy eyes

i'm afraid you're watching me
growing empty under envy
if only you knew
what your death did to me

what i never shared in group therapy

i remember in group therapy
he emphasized that not all relationships
are harmonious
that it's okay to open up
about any arguments that took place
he made it okay for me to grieve
and feel anger at the same time
i needed to know this

unlearning

**what is safe about a man
who hurts you?**

not unforgivable

you are not evil
you are not unforgivable
and i am not the womxn you fell in love with
anymore
there were times
you weren't the man i fell in love with anymore
i forgive you
for everything you didn't share with me
i forgive you everyday
we made war and we made love in the same bed
i know it wasn't healthy what we had
bound to each other against all odds
spirits connected by something like god
please forgive me
i took your pictures off the wall
i am sorry for how i survive without you

bloody sheets

the blade that cut my hair
has torn its way through my hips
and i felt numb like i wasn't there
i wish i knew beauty before i knew blood
love before i knew violence
what would i have become if i never knew fear?
i feel my words curl into my spine
as i try to make sense of everything that happened
but there are no words that exist here
you stole the meaning from my pink lips
if i could have taken your pain away
i would have driven it to the edge of the sea
and sunk it deep
like your casket in the earth
i can't believe we buried you that deep
like a secret we couldn't keep
i hold your truths like a snake
sharing secrets both sinful and sweet
telling the earth about our experiences
even the ones that made me weep deep
i breathe the blood in my sheets

caskets in my closet

today i was moving
through hangers in my closet
i forgot you were there
body in a bag
all that is left of you
preserved and untouched
i forgot you
i am moving on from you
like poems in a box
i have caskets in my closet
and i don't share you
with the world anymore
because you left mine

the greatest love

in this life i experienced you
when you died i experienced myself
the greatest love i've ever known
ends with me

september 2019

the bed of violence

i might never leave this bed
this space in time
where love was enveloping the air around us
our eyes spoke a language
that words failed to encapsulate
this moment lived on our palms
it made roots flow from our fingertips
a calmness that people mistake for numbness
it was a comfort similar to peace
and i bathed in it
this moment lives in my dreams
it is the oxygen of the night
and it is the curve of the moonlight
i embrace you tonight
spirit without body
if you hadn't died
i would have never left that space
between you and the bed
between the love and the violence
i loved you and you loved hurting me
i'm empty since you're gone
look at the scars on my hips
and tell me you didn't feel my pain
so what do you know about handling loss?
it cuts deeper than a kitchen blade
and it's a numbness that poisons your dreams
hollow moon and empty galaxy
they drained your blood
and mine spills from the cracks
you're the dead
i am the living
what we were in the beginning
we are nothing in the end
i'll never know the answers
only my dreams can travel there

to the moment we were in the hands of peace
the atmosphere of love
only there do you touch these moon scars
and kiss these petal lips

devil gave me names

broken wrist
twisted lips
broken mind wants to lick you
body shivers underneath you
feel my kiss melting through your lips
veins pulsing blood through my hips
emptying my sins to cleanse my pain
the devil gave me different names
lilith and tonantzin
snake witch
magic evil
maybe the story is corrupted
the snake is between your legs
the poison is a
nuclear weapon of mass destruction
raping and killing our people
blood is the war over our bodies
blood is our shame
and we are still alive

poison veins

blackened earth i feel your rain
pain pulling itself out of my poison veins
words could never explain
these visions i recycle
tie me to a future i fear
so i bleed myself here

freedom scares me

**i have been alone
and i will not be the first to tell you
it isn't love that scares me
it's freedom**

heaven's hills

yesterday i went for a drive
my tires rolled over endless roads
between places we built our homes
i felt tears splitting across my cheeks
under the stars i sent a kiss into space
and i loved you like i did before
just for that moment i gave you my gratitude
and it set the moon to rest
the gravity was lifting
i remember you were once my friend too
and i miss this version of you
because of our experience
i might fall into a love that is safe
and begins with something deeper than the ocean
of sex itself

october 2019

flower in the rain

i was afraid to share you with the world
i wasn't ready for people to see
that i was hurting
to define me as broken
to judge the way i lived without you
or the way i heal my pain
i am not my trauma or my past
i am myself and that is so much more
a kind of depth you couldn't dive deep enough
to ever understand
and i don't need to be understood
this i now know
because i am enough reason to live
and there's no one holding my hand behind the wheel
or helping me carry the bags
i lost parts of myself this year
and instead of filling a space
that can't be replaced
i started from the beginning
cut my hair and painted my face
lost the shame and released these weights
now i take up more space
you gave me a joy deeper than you ever knew
and i still imagine what it would be like
if you could see me now
i'm sure you would be rooting for me
i look at the moon
and imagine it's a gift you're sharing with me
it's the only space that moves me
i love you and i let you go

**a little bit more every day
freedom is the deepest love i've ever known**

under the waves

the way i loved you deep
like the ocean couldn't speak

fear of diving deep

did you take that love and sink it deep?
deprive it of oxygen?
were you afraid you might break again?
do you dance in order to bend?
and maybe you crave the feeling
wishing the waves were touching you
but they are sleeping and still
what grows under stillness
is similar to toxicity and fear
eats you alive and so you bury it deep
safety is something you never knew
so you fear what is unknown
and you created these walls
so nothing hurts you now
if love wasn't painful
we would dive deep for that kind of love

closure to create

grief is a pill i take everyday
since you died
i relapse
wishing there was enough air
to breathe you back to life
i dream of prescription drugs
everywhere i look you're hiding from me
you're burying the truth deeper than you
i went into the underworld with you
trying to bring the truth out of your veins
but all you do is bleed
and i felt the hands
pulling me into the darkness
i want to travel through dimensions
collide into planets
explode amongst the stars
burn into the sun
make love in venus flames
release sorrow like rain
plant flowers in my earth garden
pull the beauty from the moon
dance erupts from my whole body
my womb is hot water
bathe in me
feel that there is life in me
no drug could ever touch me
i won't let the pain own me
it is mine
how i endure pain
allows me to alchemize it
i birth endless cycles

silent space

you never liked words the way i did
so you left none
and that is the silence you left me in
it takes up so much space
i have to fill it

mirrors

i saw the dark entity
released my fear
faced my darkness
my shadow mirroring me
i am afraid of myself
that is fear
to heal what has been pushed
into the corners of the mind
to love what we are afraid to love

broken atmosphere

the truth is i'm sad
and then i'm mad
and i wanna break down the sky
just to meet you
because i would freeze and let go of oxygen
just to see you on the moon
and i would love you
even if i died without you
and i wanna break the earth just to touch you
darling please
can't you see i'm living without you?
this wasn't the plan
the darkness of this life

crystal pillows

i sleep with crystals by my pillow
hoping to leave darkness outside my window
i want to heal my trauma
and tend to my pain
my scars are like poems
you could never read

make me naked

your words undress my thoughts

time of the month

eat it like a pomegranate
bloody

sickle cell anemia

blood was your poison
it was my internal shame
hooked by your iv
blood, the violent cycle
running life through unborn veins

november 2019

is it cheating if he is dead?

i dreamt he broke my bed
a sledgehammer for the dead
i see the duct tape wrapped around the leg
he splits us up
and i now know that you know
someone else is breaking my bed

rejection

i dreamt that for safety
i put my face in the center of your chest
blankets wrapped around us
i felt safe
i asked you if this was okay
and you said yes
but please don't fall in love with me

numbness

i make people feel things
feeling makes people distance
themselves from me
so i feel nothing now and like that
i make people feel like nothing to me
and nothing can hurt me anymore

hope is born here

i'm sitting in a cafe
and like a an ocean wave
i come flooding apart
i am remembering
and the pain is so overwhelming
my first instinct is to cut it out of me
i've learned how easy it is
to just disappear
to go numb under the wave
to have lived in her body
to have seen through her eyes
and under your covers
to have felt her cuts and bruises
when shards of the past come back to life
i try to erase her existence
erase the trauma that lives in me
and when i call the suicide hotline
i begin to understand that cutting her out of me
will not end my pain
because trauma is not who she is
it is what she experienced
and despite all options for escape
she lives and she is alive
and that alone changes the atmosphere
she can feel that hope is born here

mercury retrograde

like a river i bathe you
like an ocean i fuck you
like a moon i pull you
like a star i burn you
volcano uterus bleeds
mercury retrograde leaves
mountain breasts feed milk to trees
flowers taste like honey and lavender
earth womxn you take the form of many bodies
loving you scares me
you are both the absence of light
and its existence
trauma can't separate those realms
you are the depth i am in search of
as i pull back the layers of the divine
there i find a humxn inside
the child within the shadows of my mind
could i not cover her eyes?
i love who you are
rather than who you wish to become

nudes

you say don't run for office
this country would never vote for a leader
whose nudes were released
you say that my body
is something to be ashamed of
but you
america
taught me at a young age
that my body determined my worth
told me to lose the weight and paint my face
to please a man who doesn't know how to please me
your advertisements taught me to be sexy
and the movies told me i needed a man
don't worry about being somebody
when you're just some body
one day i realized that i love me
and that is enough
my body is abstract art
my sexuality is not confined
and my pleasure matters
and so you say i'll never be a leader
and i'll be ruined
but my body is not yours to colonize
or exploit
to shame or to sin
to rape or to violate
my body is my own
and what kind of a leader steps down
just because she was fucking humxn?

non-consensual

i have more intimacy
with ceilings and pillows
tile floors and carpets
because they are the only part
of the experience i remember
before i resented you
for breaking into the windows of my home

the bridge and the divide

the scars still red on my hips
the places you traced your fingertips
i think of how i ran and screamed
and how nobody intervened
how do you help a womxn like me?
how do you expect me to know the difference?
when this is the love i have always known

rose oil and water

and the saddest part
is that like water
i flood into spaces that sink me
into the dirt below
and then i rise until the rivers flow
and i can't decipher what's real anymore
because when i dream of you
i think i have died too

i will never be the same

they lifted his casket from the earth
and i went into full trembling terror
i haven't heard myself scream like that
since the day you died
my mind couldn't handle
seeing your body underneath the sheets
i felt the earth drag me to you
heels sinking but it wasn't you
to the depths of a kind of horror
words fail to describe
it makes me nauseous
the endless cycle
i am determined to live
so i attempt to tear it out of me
i saw the casket grew twice in size
into a block with a lock
i opened my hand to find the lock undone
my heels in the alley
i cry to my mother
i'm never going to be the same
i wake up and look how far i've come

reflections

a year ago today
i was holding onto your palms
i was leaning into your casket
the days grew grey waiting on you
we were both going to change the world
remember?
i don't know where you went

my nana

i spread white flowers on her bed
hid all of the cancer in her room
i wanted to remember her from my childhood
before the illness made its way
between our covers

salt in the water

while writing a love letter to myself
truths were uncovered
moments of my life i colored over
even if i shared my childhood with you
you were not there
i could break open the past before you
and like salt in the water
i dissolve before you
nothing i share is shameful
it happens to be my ugly truth
some find beauty in chaos
my shadows and my triggers
they are all connected you see
like a story the chapters connect me
i have seen myself and my moon phases
i understand what has led me here
i forgive myself for dismantling my own life
and i trust in who i will become

thoughts in my tea

you will open and you will close
you will love and you will lose
but one day you will love again

TBJ 2017 - 2018

-drawn by TBJ in san francisco on december 17th, 2017-

the muse

TBJ: The only person i love in this world is you.

elena: The only reason i want to live in this world is because of you.

TBJ: You are my constitution and ruler of my universe.

elena: You are the moon that pulls the tide between my thighs.

TBJ: You are my entity and the tide between your thighs initiates the sound of a million muses serenating me.

The Love I Feel for You

The love i feel for you is infinite
You are the reason of my existence

I never thought it was possible to fall so deeply in love
You are my only desire and you inspire me without restriction

The love i feel for you is pure
You are the reasoning for my life and the reasoning of my revival

I never believed in love until i met you
You are the person whom i want to build my life with

-TBJ

my wife

You are the moonlight to my sonata
You are the kindle to my fire
You are the conquistadora of my being
You are the provocation of my goosebumps
You are the love that makes me whole
You are the passion to my sex
You are the undeniable beauty of my every desire
You are my one
You are my whole
You are my love
You are my wife

Sincerely,
TBJ

Prisoner of Your Love

I'm getting used to you
Your love ignites the passion that relinquishes in my being
With every second that passes i fall more in love with you
When i'm by your side my heart cannot seize to palpitate
You are the owner of my sentiments and of my rebirth
With you i'm blessed and closer to God
You've succeeded in allowing this crazy and disillusioned man....
To be free and want to remain a prisoner of your love

Para, Elena   De, TBJ

unrequited love

You're the remedy to my pain and igniter of my passions. Although you and i may think our love is unrequited from time to time there is no arguing the pure fact that we love eachother and will forever be a unit of desire. I will do my part as i'm sure you'll continue doing yours. I vouch to continue falling in love with you over and over again my sweet Elena. You have the heart of an angel but can love me in ways the devil may only love. I'm yours as i am sure you are mine. Perhaps the words of this note cannot express my intent of describing my heart's desire to tell you how much you mean to me. Nevertheless, i prefer to show you via physical pleasure, love, and of course passion.
Sincerely-
-TBJ

Without Your Warmth

Without your warmth…..
all the veins in my body become ice,
the beat of my heart will go stagnant

As much as i try to refrain from thinking about you,
your portrait will be engraved
deeply into my chest.

I would like to go back into my illusions…
and feel your inner being
as i felt your presence grace my every limb

As much as i try to refrain from thinking about you,
your indifference will become the reason
of my solitary confinement

The distant trembles caused by your touch…..
will become obsolete
and cause me to go into detrimental <u>withdrawals</u>
without cure

Maybe the hopelessness concerning destiny
is what has caused the universe to act against the
priceless love we possess

Without your love
i will have to die and be born again in order
to understand

i only have eyes for you

ELENA,

I know that times are hard due to our current circumstances. Nevertheless, i want you to know that i remain by your side. Our love is potent and everlasting. All of our dreams and desires of getting married and having a multitude of babies will come true. I'm ready to give my life for you and be by your side once you've given me life and make me a father. I'm ready for you to bare my last name and officially become Mrs. -------. I only have eyes for you. You are the woman i always prayed for.

Sincerely,
TBJ

wrist watch

ELENA,

The time on my clock ticks for you,
You, my beloved woman of my dreams
The passion inside of me bubbles at the thought of you
You're the reason of my existence and fuel to my fire
Without you i am just a mere mortal,
but with you i am a man with a desire
and thirst to conquer the world. Please continue
to hold my hand and forever i promise to be your
loyal lover.

Sincerely,
TBJ

reason of my existence

To: Elena

I love you baby girl.
You are the reason
of my existence.

Sincerely,
TBJ

acknowledgements

i want to close this chapter of my life by honouring the man who inspired the art. Supernova is the reason i value life and believe in love. his time on earth should not be measured in the construct of time, but rather by how he lived. TBJ was truly present in every moment we shared, he was not limited by fear, he was deeply in love with this world and he wished he had more time. he was a writer and cherished books. when we first started dating, he asked me to write about us. he believed poetry was more beautiful if it conveyed the darkness of life rather than focusing solely on the light. i would like to believe that he would have cherished reading this book, but i know that he guided my hands to create this art. TBJ, thank you for loving me and for transforming my life. you are so loved. i am filled with immense gratitude for his parents who shared their home and private world with me. for allowing me to be part of a very personal and painful process in the days that followed their son's passing. for giving life to a man whose existence will forever impact the lives he touched. it is beyond a blessing to have loved your son. mom and dad, Mary Kate and John, there are not enough words it seems. there is no such thing as being prepared for something like this. i love you for believing in my dreams, for supporting my healing journey, for handling the way grief changed me, for loving me just the same. our family is so beautiful, it made all the difference being your daughter. Lydia, Julia, John Dylan, and Micah, i love you endlessly. it is the ultimate privilege being your older sister. thank you for being my joy in this life. mama and papa, Lydia and Gordy, TBJ loved you both as much as i do. your wisdom is something i truly treasure. everyday i hope to make our nana Margarita proud. dear gratitude to my high school football coach, Romo, for being there for the wins and the losses of my life and for always believing in me. you shaped me as an athlete and now as an adult facing the obstacles ahead. you were right, "a little bit of fear is a good thing." thank you for inspiring the feminist in me that i was born to be. my dear friend, Jamie, you make me brave. if it wasn't for you, i would have never introduced myself to TBJ. you have loved me all the same, from the womxn i was before TBJ and the womxn i became after he died. you make me feel understood and seen. thank you for accepting me in all of my phases. and for all the beautiful people i met along the way, you became the adventures that made me realize there is more to live for and experience. every moment we shared were seeds i watered throughout the years. thank you to my professors, advisors, and mentors throughout my life for seeing the potential in my passions and in my thoughts. you strengthened my voice on paper. if it weren't for my therapists, bereavement groups and counselors, and spiritual healers i sometimes fear i wouldn't be here now, years down the line. and there's nothing wrong with being honest. being real with myself and vulnerable with others taught me that my life was worth it. thanks to this pain i began healing wounds that went deeper than loss. (mental) healthcare matters. the pain in my mind seeped into my body and my life choices, and healing was still possible even when i couldn't see it. this book is for people like us, experiencing loss inside of us and all around us. your resilience is the essence of the life force inside of us, and it sounds like hope for those who are hurting in this world. everyday you are living is a gift to the universe, everyday you are proof that healing belongs to us. you are the reason i believe in this art. your time is spiritual. your life is worthy of transformation and love. you make this pain feel seen and heard, and ultimately you have given me peace by reading these pages. honour your life in all the forms it takes, for you are sacred.

elena pictured in the glamis sand dunes of imperial valley (july 2020)

about the author

elena lycette was born and raised in sacramento, california. she obtained her bachelor of arts in gender, sexuality and womxn's studies from the university of california, davis at the age of twenty-two during the summer of 2020. they are a queer feminist and advocate for womxn, the lgbtqia+ community, and their intersections. she played varsity football at el camino fundamental high school as a wide receiver and cornerback. they are published in *Prized Writing 2019-2020* for their piece "Boiling Oil". she is the creator of feminist fairy dust. elena is pursuing a future in political activism, law, poetry, spirituality, and healing.

www.ingramcontent.com/pod-product-compliance
Lightning Source LLC
Chambersburg PA
CBHW072007110526
44592CB00012B/1226